The Life Cycle of a
Rabbit
by Lisa Trumbauer

Consulting Editor: Gail Saunders-Smith, Ph.D.

Consultant: Bob Fay, Animal Curator
Western North Carolina Nature Center
Asheville, North Carolina

Pebble Books
an imprint of Capstone Press
Mankato, Minnesota

Pebble Books are published by Capstone Press
151 Good Counsel Drive, P.O. Box 669, Mankato, Minnesota 56002
http://www.capstone-press.com

1 2 3 4 5 6 08 07 06 05 04 03

Library of Congress Cataloging-in-Publication Data
Trumbauer, Lisa, 1963–
    The life cycle of a rabbit / by Lisa Trumbauer.
    p. cm.—(Life cycles)
    Summary: Describes the physical characteristics, habits, and stages of
development of rabbits.
    Includes bibliographical references and index.
    ISBN 0-7368-2091-4 (hardcover)
    1. Rabbits—Life cycles—Juvenile literature. [1. Rabbits.] I. Title. II. Life cycles
(Mankato, Minn.)
QL737.L32 T78 2004
599.32—dc21   2002154693

Note to Parents and Teachers

The Life Cycles series supports national science standards related
to life science. This book describes and illustrates the life cycle
of a cottontail rabbit. The images support early readers in
understanding the text. The repetition of words and phrases
helps early readers learn new words. This book also introduces
early readers to subject-specific vocabulary words, which are
defined in the Words to Know section. Early readers may need
assistance to read some words and to use the Table of Contents,
Words to Know, Read More, Internet Sites, and Index/Word List
sections of the book.

Table of Contents

Photographs in this book show the life cycle of a cottontail rabbit.

day 1

Bunny

A rabbit begins life
as a bunny in a nest.

1 week

Newborn bunnies
are blind and deaf.
They see and hear
after one week.

The bunnies are alone in the nest most of the time. They drink milk from their mother twice each day.

4 weeks

The bunnies leave the nest after a few weeks. Now they eat plants.

adult

Adult

Bunnies become adults
after five months.
Wild rabbits live for
about four years.

A female is a doe.
A male is a buck.
The doe and buck
chase each other.
The two rabbits mate.

Building the Nest

The doe uses grass
and fur from her body
to make a nest.

18

The doe gives birth to a litter of bunnies after one month. The bunnies grow quickly.

1 week

4 weeks

newborn

adult

The Life Cycle

The bunnies are the start of a new life cycle.

Words to Know

adult—an animal that is able to mate

birth—the event of being born; when a doe gives birth, she has a litter of bunnies.

fur—the soft, thick, hairy coat of an animal; rabbit fur can be brown, white, black, or tan.

life cycle—the stages of life of an animal; the life cycle includes being born, growing up, having young, and dying; wild rabbits only live a few years; hawks, owls, and foxes eat rabbits.

litter—a group of animals born at the same time to one mother; most rabbit litters have three to five bunnies; bunnies also are called kits.

mate—to join together to produce young

nest—a place built to raise young; a doe leaves her nest during the day; she comes back to feed the bunnies at night.

Read More

Gallagher, Kristin Ellerbusch. *Cottontail Rabbits.* Pull Ahead Books. Minneapolis: Lerner, 2001.

Schuh, Mari C. *Rabbits on the Farm.* On the Farm. Mankato, Minn.: Pebble Books, 2003.

Stone, Lynn M. *Rabbits Have Bunnies.* Animals and Their Young. Minneapolis: Compass Point Books, 2000.

Internet Sites

Do you want to find out more about rabbits? Let FactHound, our fact-finding hound dog, do the research for you.

Here's how:

1) Visit *http://www.facthound.com*

2) Type in the **Book ID** number: **0736820914**

3) Click on **FETCH IT**.

FactHound will fetch Internet sites picked by our editors just for you!

Index/Word List

Word Count: 129
Early-Intervention Level: 12

Editorial Credits

Sarah L. Schuette, editor; Kia Adams, series designer; Jennifer Schonborn, interior designer; Enoch Peterson, production designer; Kelly Garvin, photo researcher; Karen Risch, product planning editor

Photo Credits

Ann & Rob Simpson, 10, 20 (right)
Bruce Coleman Inc./Wolfgang Beyer, 18
Corbis/Lynda Richardson, 4, 20 (left)
Dwight R. Kuhn, cover (adult), 12, 20 (bottom)
Eda Rogers, 14
Norvia Behling, cover (bunny), 1, 20 (top)
Visuals Unlimited/Gerard Fuehrer, 6; William J. Weber, 8; W. A. Banaszew 16